Your Life Through my Eyes

MARY J. MCKINNEY

Contents

Dedication

This book is dedicated to a very close friend of mine, who lost her fight against AIDS years ago. She was a wonderful caregiver who had a love and tolerance for kids like no one else I've ever known. They were her biggest fans and she left them so full of her love. I will remember you always, my friend

"Your Life Through My Eyes" is also dedicated to everyone who has ever went through or is going through something that they feel is to much for them to bare. Hold on; keep holding on, it will get better.

A Talk with Death

MARY

What's up Death, I heard you were in the neighborhood and I wanted to have a talk with you, if you have a minute

DEATH

What is it Mary, I am a little busy, I have about a thousand stops to make today

MARY

a thousand stops! What happened, another attack over seas?

DEATH

No, that's just the average number for today; tomorrow it could be a little more or a little less

MARY

Wow! That's crazy; those many people die in a day?

DEATH

So what was it you needed to ask me Mary because I have to get going

MARY

I want to know how you feel
about what you do.

DEATH

You mean about me taking people
out of this life on to the next?

MARY

Yes

DEATH

Well you know what they say,
somebody has to do it. I feel
bad for most people and their
families, especially the kids
because they are so young. Like
yesterday I had to go by the
hospital to take a seven year
old that got shot while out in
the yard with his older brother

MARY

What happened?

DEATH

His brother was dealing drugs
and lost a lot of money in a
deal gone bad, the supplier
thought it was a set-up but it
really wasn't

MARY

And he tried to kill the guy but
accidentally shot his brother?

DEATH

Yes, that was a hard take, it
was so sad at the hospital, I
wish there was something I could
have done but it's not my call,
I had to do what I came to do

MARY

So you do have feelings, you're
not that cold hearted bastard
people make you out to be

DEATH

Sometimes I can get heartless
when it comes to the worthless
ones like rapists and murderers

MARY

So you don't have a choice in
who you have to get? Do you
know ahead of time, like who
you have to get next week or
next year?

DEATH

No Mary, I don't, I just roam
the streets day and night taking
the breath out of those bodies
that are on my list at a given
time.

MARY

Why do people look at you so
strangely when you are present?

DEATH

Because once I approach them,
they know exactly who I am and
what I come for

MARY

So how long have you been doing
this job?

DEATH

Since the beginning of time and
will be doing it until the end
of time

MARY

Did you die and come back as Death

DEATH

Listen Mary I can't answer all
your questions baby, I have to
be going now, there are so many
people waiting on me

MARY

They're probably glad you're
late, gives them a little more
time to breath

DEATH

Good day Mary, I'll see you
later

MARY

Much Later!!! Good-Bye Death

Man Plan

How many times must I beg you to stay, before you walk away...
is it to late for you and I, is this the last day...can I hope for more
from us, or should I let go...please help me understand what I do
not know...I'm sorry I had no trust in you, I'm sorry I had no faith in
you...but you've cheated on me numerous times, what else could
I do...I have no kids and she has two from you...this other girl you
claim to hate, keep knocking at my door...I've been through this
time and time, I just can't take no more...I love you so much, do
you love me...does this five year relationship just involve me...let
me know and I'll let you be, although it will be hard, I'll set you
free...

I've been saying the same thing for five years, my friends and family
say...I say it with conviction, but still I stay...the same pain I feel day
after day...why am I here, is it because you're so fine...is it because
your loving blows my mind...is it because you're tall and sexy as
hell...maybe it's because I'm under some type of spell...it feels good
to be with you 30% of the time...the other 70% I'm about to lose
my mind....we have the most wanted cars and a beautiful home...
well it's more like a house, because I'm always alone...sports bars,
clubs, card games; you attend them all...at least that's what you say
and you don't bother to call...at 5am you walk in the door, just as
you did the five days before...am I crazy, I wonder...how much more

can I take of this drama...I feel like calling my momma...but she'll just tell me to let you go, forget the cars, forget the house...she'll tell me I should be happy, because that's what life is all about...I know she's right but I promised you I wouldn't leave...besides, next week is our five year anniversary...we're going to Bahamas Island for three days, I'm ready for the time alone with my man...no phone calls from those bitches; Debra, Jody, and Ran...no phone calls from those bitches, you're my man...at least that's the plan.... but when we get back, will that plan still stand....should I try again, or is this relationship at it's end!?

Broken Heart

You broke my heart, I ask you why
You broke my heart and watch me cry
You broke my heart and show no shame
So I ask myself, am I to blame
Was my love not good enough?
Do I not deserve your trust?
Your honesty, your commitment to me
Should I set you free or let you be
I should be happy being #1, but she just had your only son
Though we've been together for years, I have none
Maybe it's my faught for choosing a career
That keeps me so busy, takes me here and there
I'm away for days, but you're away for weeks
Sometimes we don't even speak
When you finally answer the phone, after not answering
in so long
You say that you're out of town with your boys and you'll
soon be home
Is that a hicky on your neck?
You say don't try you with the body check, that's
disrespect

Sometimes this relationship I regret
But I try to be strong, try to hold on
Why? Because we've been together for so long
My heart has been broke so many times
I feel I'm about to lose me mind
The phone rings; I answer, and you're locked up
For 30 days, you'll be locked up
I've locked the doors and changed the locks
When you get out, call your Auntie house

Hold On

I'm feeling cold when I know it's hot... I'm so confused about things I forgot... I get upset when I feel disrespect... and in no time at all, I do something I regret...I love life as I know life loves me....but knowing my purpose is hard to see...I run when I should walk... I'm silent when I should talk...I'm weak when I should be strong...I know in my heart something is wrong...but how can I move on....how can I stay true...there's so much I need to do...there so much I want to do...they say it's just the beginning but I feel it's the end...my enemies are now my friends...my friends are now my enemies, but I don't mind...if I continue to keep them close, they will be kind...they will realize that I am their brother, cousin, their best friend...then they will love me till the end...then they will know that I hide from sin...I will reach out to all mankind...the orphan children ,I will make mine...the sick, I will care for...until they hurt no more... the dumb I will teach...until they understand and demand speech...the hungry I will feed...until they are no longer in need...after doing all these things I will be strong...after doing all these things, how can I do wrong...I can't because I plan to Hold On

No Respect

My son is the love of my life but he has no respect
I try to keep him from doing things he might regret
He got arrested in 2005 for trying to sell drugs
He got in a fight a year ago for trying to be a thug
I stay awake praying all night when he don't come home
After 48 hours, he's on Amber Alert, but I'm always wrong
Wrong for being a concerned parent in the first place
Wrong for trying to address his many mistakes
Wrong for calling the cops, first of all
I'm just trying to catch you son, before you fall
I hear you curse out in front of me and your brother
I call that "no respect for your mother"
Things got to change, one way or the other
I'm not giving up on you but I still have to raise your
brother
You're 16, but you want to do what grown men do
I've done all I can, the change is on you
You want to be a man at 16, then get a job and do it right
Take care of YOU, help raise your brother, and come home
at night
If not, LEAVE, have the streets, allow me peace to raise my
other son

Pray you'll be safe from JAIL and HELL; we'll see you when
you're done
You must know your disrespect is not welcome in my
home
I Love you son, I did my best; but GONE, be GROWN
And if you realize you can't make it on your own
Do better my son, and PLEASE come HOME
This time, obey the rules and keep in check
Most of all, my son, show me some respect
As a single parent who raised you on my own
I DESERVE THAT!!!!!!!!

Through My Eyes

I stand in an empty room and wonder where I am... as I look around a child appears and says his name is Sam... He cries awful tears and his arms and legs are black and blue... I drop to my knees to look in his eyes and said "what happened to you." he just stood and cried and looked at me, with no words to say...a man appeared, called out his name and took Sam away...I never saw Sam again, and I wonder why...I feel his pain through my eyes and every day I cry. I lay awake in my bed and hear my neighbors fight... loud noises hit the wall; I pray that she's alright. I'm outside early by brake of day, just like before...face disfigured, she sits in a chair outside her door...I offer her help the best I can but she says no, I love that man...love like this I don't understand...to me that's just a weak man putting on a disguise...that's what I see, through my eyes. A friend of mine just lost her brother to the system for 10 years...she was his keeper, raised him like a son, now her heart is filled with tears...she feels as if she failed him but it was not her fault...he never had time to listen to the lessons that she taught... today she went to see him and he has lost his pride ...tonight she cried and cried and cried...why am I not surprised, I feel her pain through my eyes...I feel your pain through my eyes, and every day I cry

Am I An Alcoholic?

At work by 9, and out by 5

Can't wait to get home

I didn't get too wasted last night

I didn't get that wasted last night

Went out two nights in a row

Only consumed 1/3 of the liquor at home

I remember missing work a week ago

Why? Because I lost track of time

Had so much fun at Club 69

Don't remember much

A blackout at 4am

Who drove the car, who tucked me in?

I awoke with a used condom beside my bed

A used, empty condom beside my bed

I was so sore; but who did I let in?

I promised, I swore, I swore, I promised

I promised to never do that again

But today I'm off early with 2/3 liquor left

Someone has to, it shouldn't go to waste

Ok I'll do it; why not? I bought it

Why not, it's mine, all mine

I'll only drink half and everything will be fine

Am I an alcoholic, or is this something to past time

I'll see if I can go a week with out it

I'll see if I can go a month with out it

I'll see, maybe I can; I hope I can

It's Me

I look down on all mankind

I fly with peach of mind

I love the way I sore

The smell of the great outdoors

The trees are full of leaves

If not, I leave the scene

If not, I go down south

I have friends that meet me there

It doesn't matter where

We all do the same thing

Trying to stay in the game

Trying to not get slain

By a shooter on the hunt

Looking for some lunch

Or just having fun

Trying out his gun

Will I live to see another day?

Will today be my last?

Can I still fly away?

Can I still fly as fast?

They say yesterday is gone

And tomorrow shall come

Stressing about it is wrong

What's to come, is already done

So I fly up and down, in and out

In the hottest sun, in the coldest drought

I sing my songs all day long

People who hear me, sing along

People who see me, stop and smile

It's me, and I'm here to stay for a while

Catch me if you can, I'm about to fly away

Peace, until another day

See you when I get there

But for now, I must fly away

Why I Cry

These men around me are making me sick
I see guys getting spit on, slapped, and kicked
I see guys getting stabbed with forks and shanks
The halls, the kitchen, the bathrooms stink
I was a big man on the outside
But on the inside, I've lost my pride
I feel so helpless, so weak
Some days I don't speak, eat, or sleep
I just sit on my bunk and cry
And ask myself, why me, why me, why?
My mind is filled with family and friends
Some I'll never see again
I think of the good times to get me by
But then reality sets in; again I cry
Will I ever ride a bike or drive a car?
Will I ever play ball with my son or know who his friends are?
Will I ever open the door and step foot in my mom's new house?
Will I ever meet my little sister's spouse?
Will I ever go fishing or walk the beach?
The thought of not doing these things ever again, makes me weak
I'm in prison, prison is where I am
I didn't steal or kill but prison is where I am
It's where I sit while life passes me by
I'm in prison; prison is where I am; that's why I cry

A Dream

When I hear the word gun, my body starts to shake

And I hope it's not my life that it's coming to take

When I see a fight, I 'm ready to run

because getting hit in the face, just isn't any fun

Last night I had a dream that the violence ceased

No more stealing and killing, we were living in peace

No more criminal minds, we were having a feast

The barbeque was good; the bake-beans were great

The jealousy and hate left my plate

I awoke to realize it was a mistake

My dream was just a dream and the barbeque was fake

I Remember You

In high school I was slim, about 75 plus. My legs were skinny and I had no bust...
I played no sports but I stood with my team, I was a flag girl for two years, is what I mean...I didn't like the guys because they loved to tease, not only me but the whole female scene...this one guy was nice and always had my back, he told them to shut up, as a matter of fact...he wasn't afraid when they threaten to fight, he would never let me fight... when it was dark he walked me home at night...I called him "Protector" and he was ok with that...he gave me a name too, he called me his backpack...so what, I guess that was cool...he became my best friend that year in school...he taught me to stand up for myself, and to be nobody's fool...I respect that man to this day, a friend I'll never lose. A friend I'll always love, no matter what he does. We're married now, that's how strong our relationship grew...you're my husband now, and I remember you

Where am I

Where am I going?
Help somebody help!
Why am I sliding?
Mommy tell them to stop
Why are you screaming?
What are they doing to us!
Mommy please stop screaming
Get your hands off my head
Wow! Were am I
Turn down the lights
Too much light!
Get your hands off me
Ouch! What you hit me for
I want my mommy
Wow is this my mommy
She's so beautiful
She smell so good
I love you mommy
Can I stay with you forever?
Ah, you're smiling now

MANUSCRIPT

K AND WANDA ARE THE BEST OF FRIENDS;THEY HAVE BEEN
FOR THE PAST 6 YEARS SINCE K MOVED IN WANDA'S
NEIGHBORHOOD.K HAS A 7 YEAR OLD SON (TROY), AND
WANDA'S SON (CLEE) IS 8; THEY LOVE PLAYING TOGETHER.

INTRO: HOT SUNDAY EVENING. WANDA SWEEPS OUTSIDE
       HER DOOR, SHE LOOKS UP AND NOTICE K LEANING
       ON THE RAIL.

WANDA
(Looking up)

What's up girl, what's the crazy look
for? Troy made you mad?

K

No, I have a lot on my mind, just
thinking

WANDA

Thinking about what?

K

Come up when you're done, we'll talk

WANDA

OK, give me about 10 minutes; I'm frying
some chicken for Clee

K

Good, bring me up a piece

WANDA GOES INSIDE WHILE K SITS IN A CHAIR OUTSIDE
HER DOOR. HER BOYFRIEND VELT COMES OUT AND SITS IN
THE CHAIR BESIDE HER

                        VELT
                  (*looking at K*)

So have you made up your mind? K, talk
to me please

                         K
              (*turning away from him*)

leave me alone

                        VELT

Listen K, I'm sorry, how many times do
I need to apologize? I'm sorry, it was
a big mistake

VELT HOLDS K BY THE HAND

                         K

You damn right, it was a big mistake

K SNATCHES HER HAND AWAY FROM HIM

        but how am I sure you won't make another
        big mistake. I have a child to think
        about Velt, what if you would have
        brought home something besides another
        woman's baby, like some kind of disease.
        Did you think about me while you were
        having your 10 minutes of unprotected
        sex-Huh?

                        VELT

        baby I'm sorry, that was the biggest
        mistake of my life, I love you and I
        want you to have my baby. K, I'll never
        hurt you again

        (*with a tearful look in his eyes*)

Please keep the baby

                         K

You just had a baby from Keysha; Velteese
she's a year old- remember?

VELT

So you'll have my son, and Troy will
have a little brother to play with. You
were raised better K; you can't get rid
of the baby, it's not his fault.

K

(smiling)

she's not a he

VELT

(excited and smiling)

thank you K, you just made me the
happiest man in the world and I promise
to stand by you no matter what. I love
you girl.

WANDA IS WALKING UP THE STEPS WITH A PLATE OF FOOD
IN HER HAND AS VELT IS GIVING K A BIG HUG

WANDA

(hands K the plate)

did I miss something, what are we
celebrating. I hope that's a goodbye
hug, it's about time you get rid of
this jerk

K

no Wanda, as a matter of fact it's bad
news

(smiling at Velt)

girl you got to sit down for this one

WANDA

(giving Velt a push on the shoulder)

Get up jerk, go make yourself useful

VELT STANDS UP AND GIVES K A KISS ON THE FOREHEAD

VELT

baby you need to pick better friends,
this ones got flees

(reaching for the plate)

and I wouldn't eat that if I were you

WANDA SHAKES HER HEAD AS VELT GOES INSIDE TO WATCH
THE GAME, K LAUGHS

WANDA

So what's up girl, what's going on?

K

OK; you remember I told you that Velt
and I were using condoms every since I
found out about his baby from Keisha

WANDA

Yes

(looking confused)

K

well I lied- I'm pregnant

WANDA
(surprised)

What!! Are you serious?

K

I wish I wasn't

WANDA

that's great K, you two are the best. I
know Velt did you wrong with that slut
Keysha, but I'm glad you worked it out.
He's so good to you and Troy, and I do
believe he hates what he did to you.

K

I know, but what if he would have brought
AIDS home Wanda- what then?

WANDA

well thank God he didn't, and you gave
him another chance

(giving K a hug)

I'm so happy for you guys. Jake and
I have been trying for months, what's
your secret?

K

maybe it's the Geritol Vitamins I've been taking lately

WANDA

I've heard that somewhere- I'll bye some today at the grocery store, what time are we going shopping?

K

you're serious huh?

WANDA

as serious as a heart attack

BOTH GIRLS BEGIN TO LAUGH; VELT COMES TO THE DOOR

VELT

baby do you want me to fix you something to eat?

  (reaching for the plate in K's hand)

because I don't want you to eat anything that will harm the baby

WANDA

very funny animal, now go back to your cage

K
(laughing)

no thanks baby, I'm going to eat Wanda's chicken

VELT

let us pray

  (Velt and K bow their heads)

INTRO: SUPERMARKET. LATER THAT DAY WANDA AND K ARE WALKING THE AISLES SHOPPING FOR BARGAINS WHEN KURT (A HANDSOME HOMOSEXUAL FRIEND OF K'S) WALKS UP. HE SMELLS AND DRESS SO WELL.

K

what's up Kurt?

WANDA

what's up Kurt, are you lifting weights?
you look a little buffed

KURT

no girl

(modeling around Wanda)

It's just in me to look this good

WANDA

yel right

KURT

don't hate

WANDA

please

KURT
(jokingly)

and tell your man to stop eye-balling
me, he's not my type

WANDA

you wish

KURT

No I don't

(shaking his head)

he's broke, you can keep him

WANDA

K let me go find my Geritol, before I
kill Kurt

KURT

Whatever girlfriend; you need more than
Geritol for those skinny legs

WANDA WALKS AWAY TALKING UNDER HER BREATH, K IS
LAUGHING

K

you two are crazy

KURT

No she's crazy. So what's been going on
girl, I haven't seen you at the club
lately. What you wifie now?

                    K
No, but I am pregnant

                  KURT
               (*shocked*)
What!!

               (*smiling*)
well it's about time

                    K
So what do you think?

                  KURT
I think that's great, and with that fine
ass man of yours; you two will make
a beautiful baby. Despite his faults,
he's a good man K, and he fits right into
fatherhood for Troy. No one will ever
replace Big Troy, God bless his soul;
but he's gone, and Velt fits right into
that space.
          (*rubbing K's belly*)
you're going to have a baby

                    K
speaking of babies, are you still seeing
that kid from Newark?

                  KURT
Oh, I meant to tell you, his little

fine ass got married on me

                    K
What! To who? To what?

                  KURT
his baby momma, he felt it was the right
thing to do since she had his child.
He called me last week wanting to come
over, I told him I'm done with men;
girl they lie too much.

> *(shaking his head)*

Do you believe he's been married for over 5 months now, and I just found out two weeks ago, when I saw the wedding picture in his wallet

K

Oh well, you'll get over it; he was too young for you anyway

KURT

he's twenty one K, that's not too young; hell I'm only thirty. forget him, I'm leaving anyway

K

Leaving!

> *(surprised look)*

Where are you going?

KURT

away from here, I'm sick of this place. But don't worry; you'll be the first to know

K

> *(sounding upset)*

but I don't want you to go

KURT

I don't want to leave either, but I have to

WANDA WALKS TOWARDS THEM WITH A HANDFUL OF ITEMS

WANDA

Old man you still here. Stop harassing my friend. There's a sale on tampons on aisle four

THEY ALL START LAUGHING, EVEN KURT AS HE WALKS AWAY

KURT

K, I'll call you later in the week

Mary J. Mckinney

                              K

alright Kurt

                            KURT
                    (turning the corner)

and Wanda the flea powder is on aisle
five

                           WANDA
                      (K is laughing)

that's not funny

                              K

Oh yes it is, I have noticed you
scratching a lot lately

                           WANDA

Girl I almost told you something. Did
you get everything you needed?

                              K

I believe so

                           WANDA

well let's go. I have to start on my
baby medicine.

                              K

you really are serious

                           WANDA

yes girl, I can't have you walking
around with a big belly by yourself

TWO WEEKS LATER K IS LYING ON THE COUCH WATCHING
TV. SHE HAS NOT BEEN FEELING WELL THROUGHOUT HER
PREGNANCY.

THERE'S A KNOCK AT THE DOOR.

                              K
                       (yells out)

Troy! – come get the door

TROY YELLS OUT WHILE APPROACHING THE LIVING ROOM

                    TROY

Who is it?

                    CLEE

It's me

                    TROY
            (Unlocks the door)

Oh what's up Clee, you come over for me
to whoop you in some Madden?

                    CLEE

OK, we'll see who really got game. Hello
Ms. K

                     K

Hey Clee, you finish your homework?

                    CLEE

Yes mam

                     K

What's your momma doing?

                    CLEE

frying some pork chops

                    TROY
          (yells from his bedroom)

Come on Clee and pick your team!

                     K

That's right; go let my son teach you
a lesson

                    CLEE
          (walks towards the bedroom)

We'll see who comes out crying

K DRIFTS OFF TO SLEEP, BUT IS AWAKEN ABOUT AN HOUR
AND A HALF LATER BY THE PHONE RINGING; SHE ANSWERS
IT

                     K
              (sleepy voice)

Hello

                                      Mary J. Mckinney

                    WANDA
sorry girl I didn't mean to wake you.
you've been sleeping all week

                      K
I know girl, this baby got me so tired.

So what have you been up to?

                    WANDA
Trying to make a baby. I was ovulating
this week so I've been locking Jake in
the house for the last couple of days

                      K
What! you kept that man in the house?

                    WANDA
                  (laughing)
I had to hide his keys for two days. Girl
you want some pork-chop and vegetables?

                      K
No, Velt is bring Chinese food on his
way from work; besides I haven't been
able to hold much down, everything
smells funny

                    WANDA
So I see you forgot all about the misery
that comes with having a baby

                      K
Yel girl, you sure you want to do this?

                    WANDA
Oh Yes!
                (they both laugh)
K, tell Clee to come down and eat, so
he can get ready for bed

                      K
OK, he'll probably be glad to be rescued
from Troy kicking his butt on that game.
So I'll call you tomorrow

                    WANDA
OK girl feel better

THEY BOTH HANG UP THE PHONE

> **K**
> *(yells out)*

Clee! It's time to go home, your dinner
is ready

> **CLEE**
> *(upset)*

your son is a cheater, how can he win
three games in a row?

> **TROY**

Get out loser; I almost feel bad beating
you like that.

> **CLEE**

Whatever; good night Ms. K

> **K**

Good night Clee, better luck next time

THE WEATHER WAS VERY BAD OVER THE NEXT WEEK. CLEE
STAYED OVER, AND TROY BEAT HIM AND VELT IN MADDEN
ALL WEEKEND. K GOT PLENTY OF REST.

INTRO: IT'S A BEAUTIFUL MONDAY MORNING THE SUN IS
SHINNING AFTER ALMOST TWO WEEKS OF STORMS.
K IS DOWN THE HALL WAVEING AT TROY AND CLEE
AS THEY GET ON THE SCHOOL BUS. WHILE WALKING
BACK TO HER APARTMENT THE PHONE RINGS, SHE
HURRIES IN TO ANSWER IT.

> **K**

Hello

> **NURSE**

Hello, may I speak to K?

> **K**

This is she; may I ask who's calling?

> **NURSE**

Yes, my name is Nicky Lay and I'm a
nurse at Cross Hospital. Your friend
Kurt Taylor was admitted last Friday

evening, and he asked me to give you a
call today

                    K
                (nervous)
What happened! Is he OK?

                NURSE NICKY
Well he's not doing too good, will you
be able to come over

                    K
I'll be there in thirty minutes

                NURSE NICKY
I'll speak with you when you get here

K HANGS UP THE PHONE AND QUICKLY GETS DRESSED AND
OUT THE DOOR

INTRO: 25 MINUTES LATER AT CROSS HOSPITAL. K WALKS
       TO THE INFORMATION DESK WITH A PUZZLED LOOK
       ON HER FACE THAT SHE HAD WORN SINCE SHE HUNG
       UP THE PHONE.

                RECEPTIONIST
Good morning, may I help you?

                    K
Yes, I'm here to see Nurse Nicky Lay

                RECEPTIONIST
and you must be K?

                    K
Yes

                RECEPTIONIST
        (pointing towards the waiting area)
have a seat right over there and I'll
page Nurse Nicky for you

                    K
Thank you

K WALKS OVER TO THE WAITING ROOM WHERE THERE'S
A BEAUTIFUL YOUNG LADY SITTING ACROSS FROM HER
CRYING. A FEW MINUTES LATER A FRIENDLY NURSE WALKS
OVER TO SHAKE K'S HAND.

                    NURSE NICKY
     Hi K, I'm Nurse Nicky

                         K
     Hi

                    NURSE NICKY
          (*turning to the crying woman*)
     Hi, and you must be Judy

                       JUDY
          (*trying to pull herself together*)
     Yes

                    NURSE NICKY
     ladies follow me

THE TWO FOLLOW NURSE NICKY DOWN THE HALL AND INTO
HER OFFICE

     Have a seat please
               (*She closes the door*)

                         K
     What's wrong with Kurt?

JUDY SHAKES HER HEAD AS IF SHE DON'T WANT TO HEAR
THE ANSWER TO THAT QUESTION

                    NURSE NICKY
     Kurt has triple pneumonia, his immune
     system is badly damaged, and...

                         K
          (*confused and interruptive*)

     what are you talking about, I just saw
     him a couple weeks ago and he looked
     fine to me.

K IS BEGINNING TO TEAR UP BECAUSE JUDY WON'T STOP
CRYING

                                    Mary J. Mckinney

NURSE NICKY

On the outside, but on the inside the AIDS has taken over

K
(shocked)

AIDS!?

JUDY

I don't believe it, how can he be gay, I just can't believe it, he's apart of me and I love him so much

K
(looking even more confused)

You two were lovers?

JUDY
(talking through tears)

No, I just moved here less than a year ago; he and my husband are lovers. I waited two years to be married, and this is what I get. I have a son to live for, a little baby boy who needs me

(crying out)

Why me, why me

NURSE NICKY REACHES OUT AND GIVES JUDY A HUG

NURSE NICKY

Judy you need to get tested, please don't upset yourself. There's a lot of help out here if you need it; let's take this one step at a time, OK?

(rubs Judy's back)

Come with me Judy, we'll get you tested and have a counselor speak with you. Come with us K.

THE THREE LADIES WALK DOWN THE HALL, K NOW KNOWS THAT THIS IS THE WIFE OF THE YOUNG MAN THAT KURT WAS TELLING HER ABOUT, SHE IS SPEECHLESS.

(stopping in front of a lab door)

K, give me two minutes, let me walk
Judy in

JUDY TAKES IN A DEEP BREATH AND EXHALES; SHE
MAKES EYE CONTACT WITH K AND SEES THAT K IS CRYING
SILENTLY. JUDY TURNS TO GIVE HER A HUG, THE TWO
EMBRACE FOR WHAT SEEMED LIKE FOREVER

                         K
God bless you Judy, I pray that you'll
be OK

                       JUDY
It was nice meeting you K, but please
tell your friend that I don't think
he's a nice person at all. He lives
with a deadly virus and does nothing to
protect others from getting infected

                         K
He didn't know Judy, he just found out
about the marriage a few weeks ago

                       JUDY
Good bye K

                         K
Bye Judy

NICKY AND JUDY WALK IN THE LAB ROOM. K STANDS
AGAINST THE WALL RUBBING HER STOMACH AS SHE CRY
SILENTLY. THE LAB DOOR OPENS AND NURSE NICKY COMES
OUT.

                    NURSE NICKY
                (checking her pager)
Let me take you to see Kurt now, and
remember he is in a lot of pain, not so
much physically but mentally

                         K
How did Judy find out about Kurt?

                    NURSE NICKY
In the worst way

                (shaking her head)

                                    Mary J. Mckinney

Kurt called her house to speak with her husband about his condition, they both picked up at the same time. Her husband begins talking with Kurt, and she decided to listen, with them not knowing she too was on the phone.

> (shaking her head again)

She said that she just started trembling. She called the number back after they hug up and I answered. She was hysterical, and said she needed to get tested right away

K

God help her, she's so young

NURSE NICKY

And so is her husband, but AIDS don't discriminate; it doesn't care how old or young you are, nor how rich or poor

K

what I don't understand is why so many men are gay?

NURSE NICKY

That is yet to be determined k; do you have kids?

K

Yes, a little boy, and I'm expecting

> (rubbing her stomach)

hoping for a girl

NURSE NICKY

I see congratulations; have you been tested?

K

Yes, last month was our third test, everything was fine

NURSE NICKY

Good. Take care of yourself and your children, spend time with them, go to their schools, know their friends, and

if you don't approve of them, don't
let them hang out together. Get them
involved in community activities like
sports, church, you know what I mean?

(K knobs her head)

Teach them about the dangers of
unprotected sex and its consequences,
encourage them to wait; education first

K

Yes, I understand Nurse Nicky

NURSE NICKY
(stopping)

OK, we're here. It was nice to meet you
K, take care

K

Thanks Nurse Nicky, but when do you
think he'll be released?

NURSE NICKY

I don't know, his T-cells are really
low, his immune system is severely
damaged, but anything is possible, it's
all up to him

K

Thanks again Nurse Nicky, you have a
blessed day

NURSE NICKY

You too K

K ENTERS THE ROOM AFTER PUTTING ON THE FACE MASK
AND GOWN REQUIRED ENTERING THE ROOM. SHE IS SHOCKED
TO SEE KURT LOOKING TWENTY POUNDS THINNER THAN HE
DID THE OTHER WEEK, AND HE'S HOOKED UP TO A MACHINE
WITH AN OXYGEN MASK ON HIS FACE.K WALKS OVER AND
STANDS NEAR THE BED WHERE HE SEEMS TO BE SLEEPING.
AFTER OBSERVING HIM FOR A COUPLE MINUTES, KURT
SLOWLY TURNS AND OPENS HIS EYES

KURT
(Slowly removing the mask from his face)

What's up girl?

Mary J. Mckinney

K

(with a sad look)

Kurt

KURT

K listen, before you say anything. I had an Ideal I was HIV positive years ago; my x-lover died from AIDS about five years ago, that's when I moved here

(pausing to breath in the oxygen mask)

James and I had stopped seeing each other about a year or so before his death, so I put him out my mind, I didn't think about it, I never got tested. A couple years after his death I started feeling weak and tired all the time, I broke out in rashes that wouldn't go away, but still I wouldn't get tested.

(he begins coughing uncontrollably; K gives him a drink of water)

K, I didn't think it could happen to me, not me, I'm a good hearted person. I wouldn't wish this on my worst enemy

K

Kurt, AIDS is not prejudice, it doesn't care who you are, it comes to kill and destroy. Absentee is 100%, condoms are less than that, but necessary if you are going to have sex

KURT

K, I'm scared, I don't want to die, but I'm not sure I want to stay either, not in this condition

(crying)

I called my friend, Mr. Newark, he wanted to come see me but I told him not to

K

(hesitant)

Kurt

                    KURT

What is it?

                     K

His wife heard your conversation over
the phone; she was here at the hospital.
She is so afraid

                    KURT
           (slowly shaking his head)

No, I want them to stay together; he
really wants his family life. I truly
think he can change

                     K

What about...

                    KURT
              (interrupting)

K, his wife is going to be OK, he is the
safest man I've ever been with, and he
would never hurt his family like that

                     K
             (sighing in relief)

Thank God, I felt so bad for her, she
wouldn't stop crying

                    KURT
            (turning his head away)

Neither can I

                     K

You must stay strong Kurt, keep fighting
please, don't give up on me. I'll come
back to see you everyday, until you
come home.

                    KURT

Thanks K

                     K

Is there anyone you would like for me
to call, your mother maybe?

                    KURT

No, I'll wait till I get out; I don't
want her to worry

                                    Mary J. Mckinney

K

You sure Kurt

KURT

I'm tired, could you just sing my favorite song before you go

(puts his mask back on)

Sure Kurt

K BEGINS TO SING SOFTLY AS SHE STROKES KURT HAND. BY THE TIME SHE REACHES THE END OF THE SONG KURT IS FAST ASLEEP.K WISPIER IN HIS EAR "I LOVE YOU KURT" THEN GIVES HIM A KISS ON THE FOREHEAD BEFORE LEAVING.

INTRO: LATER THAT EVENING, K, TROY, AND VELT ARE AT THE TABLE HAVING DINNER WHEN SOMEONE KNOCKS CRAZY HARD AT THE DOOR.

TROY
(getting up from the table)

Who is it?

WANDA

(sounding excited)

Me!

TROY
(opening the door)

Hi Ms. Wanda, we were having dinner.

(yelling towards the kitchen)

Mom! Ms. Wanda is here

WANDA

What's up Troy, dinner smells good, what is it?

TROY
(walking towards the kitchen)

mash potato and meat loaf

K

No you can't have any

(smiling jokingly)

What's up Wanda, where have you been? I
tried calling you today

> **WANDA**
> *(excited)*

Guess what K?

> **K**

What's up with you girl, are you on
something?

> **VELT**

She's been on something for years, I'm
surprised you didn't notice baby

VELT AND TROY START LAUGHING AS THEY GIVE EACH
OTHER A HIGH FIVE LEAVING THE KITCHEN

> **WANDA**

Don't let that man's boring sense-of-
humor rub off on Troy.

> *(shaking her head)*

anyway girl, you got to stand up for
this

> **K**
> *(cleaning the table)*

I'm standing, what is it?

> **WANDA**

Well sit down. K, I told you that I
wouldn't let you go through this alone,
so I've decided to join you

> **K**

What are you talking about crazy girl?

> **WANDA**

I'm pregnant!

> **K**
> *(smiling)*

What! Are you serious?

> **WANDA**

As serious as a heart attack. Just took
the test

SHE PULLS A ZIP-LOCK BAG FROM HER BACK POCKET,
CONTAINING A POSITIVE PREGNANCY TEST STICK. THEY
HUG, LAUGH, AND DANCE AROUND IN THE KITCHEN UNTIL
VELT WALKS IN AND ORDERS WANDA TO GET OUT.

IT'S EARLY THE NEXT MORNING, K IS UPSTAIRS AT THE
RAIL WATCHING TROY AND CLEE AT THE BUS STOP, WHEN
WANDA COMES UP THE STAIRS.

K

So how you feeling momma?

WANDA

OK, I guess

K

So, what did Jake have to say?

WANDA

Last night after I took the test, he
asked if he could finally leave the
house, but he didn't; now I can't get
rid of him

(they both laugh)

give me the number to your doctor, and
from now on we can car pool

K
(looking distant)

Cool

TROY
(getting on the bus)

Bye mom

K

Bye baby, have a good day

CLEE
(yelling out)

Bye mom

WANDA

Later Clee, be good.

(turning towards K)

What's wrong K? What's on your mind?

> **K**
> *(taking a deep breath)*

Wanda I hate to rain on your parade, but I have a friend in the hospital, and he's not doing too well

> **WANDA**

Who?

> **K**

Kurt

> **WANDA**

Fine ass Kurt, what happened to him?

> **K**

He has AIDS

> **WANDA**
> *(A look of disbelief)*

No not Kurt, we just say him K, he looked OK

> *(staring at K)*

Did you know this?

> **K**

I had no idea Wanda; I was as shocked as you when Nurse Nicky called yesterday

> **WANDA**

So you've seen him?

> **K**

Yes, he's so weak and frail. I never believed that someone could change so much in such a short time. He got caught in the rain the other week and caught the flu, now he's in the hospital with triple pneumonia.

> **WANDA**

Triple pneumonia, that's terrible K

> *(still in disbelief)*

He looked so healthy, who could have known, he has such a great personality.

Mary J. Mckinney

> (silence)

So when are you going back to see him

K

today, and again tomorrow morning after
I leave the doctor

WANDA

I can't go today but I'll go with you
tomorrow. I have an appointment at HRS.
I'll make my doctor's appointment while
I sit at the doctor with you tomorrow.

K

OK

> (walking towards her door)

I'm going to lie back down for a little
while; I didn't get much sleep last
night

WANDA

I'm so sorry about Kurt

K

Me too girl, I feel so bad for him

IT'S AFTER 12PM, WANDA RETURNS HOME TO FIND JAKE AND
HIS FRIEND LUTHER IN HER LIVING ROOM SMOKING MARIJUANA

WANDA
> (very upset)

Jake, haven't I told you not to smoke
in the house!?

JAKE

baby it's early, and Clee is not due
home for a few hours; and besides, I
bought your favorite house spray

> (pointing at the can on the table)

Please sit down, you shouldn't upset
yourself, it's not good for the baby

LUTHER

Oh congratulation Wanda! Jake told me
the good news; actually, that's what
we're celebrating

WANDA GIVES THEM BOTH AN EVIL LOOK; TEN WALKS BACK
OUT THE DOOR. SHE CAN HEAR LUTHER LAUGHING AS SHE
WALKS AWAY. WANDA HEADS UPSTAIRS; SHE CAN HEAR K'S
PHONE RINGING AS SHE APPROACHES THE DOOR. K SEE'S
WANDA AND OPENS THE DOOR AS SHE ANSWERS THE PHONE.

K

Hello

NURSE NICKY

Hi K, it's Nurse Nicky from The Cross
Hospital

K

Yes Nurse Nicky is everything OK; tell
Kurt I'll be there soon.

WANDA LOOKS WORRIED AS SHE SIT ON THE COUCH AND
LOOK AT K AS SHE TALKS TO NURSE NICKY ON THE PHONE

NURSE NICKY

I'm sorry K, but Kurt didn't make it
through the night, he's gone

(silence)

K, K are you still there

K
(eyes fill with tears)

How could this happen so fast?

WANDA WALKS OVER TO K AND RUBS HER BACK, AS SHE TRY
TO HOLD BACK HER OWN TEARS

NURSE NICKY

He got tired of the fight; he stopped
taking his medication weeks ago. He
gave up K, I'm sorry. Do you know how
to contact any of his family members?
He denied having anyone but you and a
little sister in Georgia

K

His family didn't approve of his
lifestyle, so he left home years ago

Mary J. Mckinney

NURSE NICKY

We did contact Georgia authorities; they haven't gotten back with us. If you know anyone, could you please have them give me a call?

K

I have a spare key to his apartment; I'll stop by there and see what I can find

NURSE NICKY

That would be helpful. He had the nurse write him a letter yesterday after you left; the letter is for you K, so please stop by and pick it up. I'll see you when you get here OK, and again, I'm sorry about your friend, he seemed to be a very nice person

K HANGS UP THE PHONE AND WANDA GIVE HER A HUG

K AND WANDA ARRIVE AT THE HOSPITAL AFTER LEAVING KURT'S APARTMENT. K FOUND MANY LETTERS FROM KURT'S LITTLE SISTER; SHE BROUGHT THE ONES WITH HER THAT CONTAINED PHONE NUMBERS. FROM THE LETTERS, IT SEEMED THAT KURT'S FAMILY LOVED HIM DEEPLY; HIS MOTHER WAS JUST DISAPPOINTED BECAUSE SHE WANTED A DIFFERENT LIFE FOR HIM THAN THE ONE HE CHOSE.

WANDA
(approaching the front desk)

excuse me

RECEPTIONIST
yes, may I help you?

WANDA
yes we're here to see Nurse Nicky

RECEPTIONIST
have a seat, I'll page her

K
(sitting)

I hate hospitals, they give me the creeps, and people are always dying here

WANDA

I know

NURSE NICKY WALKS UP

NURSE NICKY

Hi K, glad you could make it, again I'm sorry

K

Thank you Nurse Nicky

(turning to Wanda)

I would like you to meet my best friend Wanda

NURSE NICKY

Hi Wanda, pleased to meet you

(she hands K an envelope)

I believe this is for you

K

Thank you and I have a couple of numbers for you

NURSE NICKY

Great! I'll try them now, give me a minute

NURSE NICKY WALKS AWAY. K AND WANDA HAVE A SEAT ON A COUCH IN THE WAITING AREA. K OPENS THE LETTER AND BEGINS TO READ IN A LOW VOICE, WANDA SITS CLOSE AND LISTENS

K

(THE LETTER)

Hi K; or should I say good bye. First I must tell you that you were my best friend. I will pray for you tonight and wish for you and Velt to have a healthy baby that looks like the both of you because you both are beautiful.

I'm going to miss you, my mother, and my little sister; please let them know how much they meant to me. I was

Mary J. Mckinney

raised so much better than this; I don't
know what happened to me. I hate most
of all, what I've done to my mother
because she told me long ago that "no
mother wants to bury her child." AIDS
is killing so many of us, at a rate
that is unbelievable. You stay safe K
and tell your hot ass friend Wanda to
protect herself too, even though she's
a little off. I must rest now my friend;
I'll see you in the next life; live
long and be happy.

Love always;

your friend Kurt Taylor

K AND WANDA HUG EACH OTHER AS THEY CRY SILENTLY.
NURSE NICKY WALKS TOWARD THEM

K
(wiping her tears)

So did you get in touch with anyone?

NURSE NICKY

Yes, his mother: she was hysterical.
She blames herself for not standing by
him, she truly loved her son. I feel
bad for her because I know she wanted
to tell him that before

(Nurse Nicky shakes her Head)

This type of thing happens every day;
HIV is running through our community
at a very fast pace, especially in our
youth who lack the knowledge of the
seriousness of this disease

K

Why is it that most people don't want
to get tested?

NURSE NICKY

They'd rather not know. Some people
feel safe not knowing, that way they

can go on with their life as usual and don't have to tell anyone if they're HIV positive.

WANDA

But why do some people look so bad and others you can't even tell they're sick? Like Kurt, who would have known.

NURSE NICKY

There are numerous people living with HIV/AIDS who take care of themselves.

They take their meds, exercise, and eat right; this helps their immune system, which is attacked by the virus. Others give up; they stress themselves out with the thought that they're going to die.

WANDA

Why is this disease so widespread in the black community?

NURSE NICKY

We are not protecting ourselves as we should. Do you know how many women come through these hospital doors pregnant; some from the same man, and some from bisexual men.

WANDA

but most women don't know if there man is bisexual or not

NURSE NICKY

It can be hard, but you must pay close attention to your spouse; get to know his friends and where they hang. You can even talk to friends from his past; don't be afraid to ask questions, it's your life you're protecting; any new relationship needs to be tested for HIV/AIDS.

WANDA

This is deep

NURSE NICKY

Very deep Wanda, it's truly cutting our blacks like a knife

RECEPTOINIST

Excuse me Nurse Nicky; you're wanted in the ER

NURSE NICKY

Sorry girls, duty calls. Kurt's mom will be in town this week; I gave her your number K, so she'll be giving you a call.

(*turning to the   receptionist*)

Give them some of our brochures on HIV/ AIDS and its prevention

RECEPTOINIST

Yes mam

THE GIRLS SAY GOOD-BYE TO NURSE NICKY AND THEN FOLLOW THE RECEPTIONIST TO A SHELF FULL OF BROCHURES

IT'S 10:20AM; K AND WANDA ARE LEAVING THE DOCTORS OFFICE. K WAS GIVEN A GOOD REPORT ON HER PREGNANCY PROGRESS.

K
(*driving*)

So when is your appointment Wanda?

WANDA

I told the doctor we're twins, so I made my appointment the same time as yours

K
(*shaking her head*)

What do you want to eat this lovely morning crazy girl?

WANDA

Spoons Grill, I love their breakfast

K

sounds good. I spoke with Kurt's mother last night, she feels so guilty. I told her she had no reason to, her son loved her very much and didn't expect for her to approve of his preference.

WANDA

I feel her pain K, I felt so guilty about my mom's death. I gave her such a hard time but she never gave up on me. I felt responsible for her heart attack, but thanks to you and a lot of counseling, I'm doing better now. You moved in the neighborhood right when I needed a friend

K

I know, you went through a lot

(parking)

The funeral is in Georgia this Saturday; I need you to come with me

(pausing)

Isn't that your car?

WANDA

Jake and Luther must be here for breakfast, we'll get them to pay for our food

THE GIRLS ENTER THE RESTAURANT AND SEES JAKE AT A TABLE IN THE FAR BACK, HOLDING HANDS WITH A LOVELY YOUNG LADY. WANDA HEADS TO THE TABLE IN A RAGE, K IS ONE STEP BEHIND HER

WANDA
(angry)

Excuse me Jake! May I have a word with you please?

JAKE
(shocked)

hey Wanda baby, what are you doing here, I was just about to call you

WANDA

For what! To see where I was, so I wouldn't run into you

THE YOUNG LADY AT THE TABLE GETS UP TO LEAVE

WANDA

No, you don't have to Leave, I'm sorry for Being so rude

(holding out her hand)

I'm Wanda, Jake's fiancé and soon to be baby momma

YOUNG LADY
(surprised)

I'm sorry, I didn't know

(standing and turning to Jake)

You told me you were different from my ex-husband, liar!

SHE DASHES HER TEA IN JAKE'S FACE AND WALKS AWAY

WANDA

You have 15 minutes to get to the apartment

K AND WANDA LEAVE THE RESTAURANT

K
(at the car)

Are you ok girl?

WANDA

No, but I will be when I get his shit out my apartment. That's it K, it's over, it should of been over a long time ago

IT'S SUNDAY EVENING, K AND WANDA ARE IN A CAB RETURNING HOME FROM THE AIRPORT; THEY JUST HAD A SAD, BUT EXCITING WEEKEND IN GEORGIA.

WANDA

Kurt sure had a lot of friends; it's
hard to believe he left home, everyone
seem so friendly there

K

His little sister looks just like him;
she took it hard, they spoke on the
phone every week, she said he was her
best friend, he told her he was moving
far away and wouldn't be able to talk
to her as often; it was then that I
remembered our conversation in the
supermarket. He said he was moving even
though he didn't want to, but had to;
he had given up then. I thought he was
trying to get away from Mr. Newark; I
should have paid more attention

WANDA

There's no way you could have known K,
that day he was the healthiest looking
man in the world. I'm going to miss him

K

Me to Wanda, I miss him already.

(reaching for her phone)

I better call Velt to let him know we're
on our way home

K CALLS AND TALK WITH VELT FOR A FEW MINUTES

WANDA

Is everything OK?

K

Yes, they're at the movies. He said the
boys wanted to watch different movies so
they decided to watch them both. The
second one just started

WANDA

Good, I can go home and take a nap.

K

You probably have a hundred missed calls
from Jake

Mary J. Mckinney

WANDA

I know. That bum, he just needs somewhere
to stay, not at my door, it's over for
him; and besides, Kurt's fine cousin is
coming to see me next week, he's so cute

K

He is cute; I see why Curt was so fine;
it runs in his family. but Wanda…

(serious)

I don't think it's wise to let this man
come visit you so soon; you don't know
him like that

WANDA

(smiling)

Oh yes I do. I'm a big girl K; I can
take care of myself, thank you

K

I know you can, I just want you to be
careful and protect yourself

WANDA

Look who's talking about protection

K

that's right me, a pregnant woman whose
man and herself have taken several
AIDS test since Velt cheated on me,
thank God they all came back negative.
Velt was so scared after sleeping with
Keysha; I found a negative HIV test of
his from the clinic, which he took when
Keysha was about three months pregnant

WANDA

(shocked)

What! And you never told me

K

I never told anyone, not even Velt. He
was so distant the months before that,
I thought it was me; maybe I gained too
much weight, or he just didn't love
me anymore; but it was because he was

trying to protect me from his mistake.

He really messed up Wanda, but I feel in
my heart that he'll never do it again,
every day I pray for strength in our
relationship

WANDA

It's sad that after one night with that
slut, the baby was still proven to be
his; then again it only takes one time

K

As easy as contracting AIDS

WANDA

enough with this AIDS foolishness,
you're making me sick

WANDA REACHES INTO HER PURSE AND HANDS THE CAB
DRIVER THE FEE AS HE STOPS IN FRONT OF THE APARTMENT
COMPLEX. K PULLS MONEY OUT TOO AND GIVES HIM A BIG
TIP

CAB DRIVER

Thank you ladies

WANDA

That's for listening to our life story
on the way

THE CAB DRIVER GETS THE GIRLS LUGGAGE OUT THE
TRUNK, WANDA ROLLS HER'S TO HER DOOR. THE DRIVER
CARRIES K'S LUGGAGE UP STAIRS

WANDA

Keep Clee over there for a while, I'll
call you when I get up

K IS IN THE KITCHEN COOKING BOILED CHICKEN, YELLOW
RICE AND VEGETABLES WHEN VELT AND TROY WALKS IN.
TROY RUNS OVER TO HUG HER

TROY

Hi mom, we saw two good movies

                              K
So I heard, did you miss me?

                            TROY
Yep

                            VELT
                          (Kissing)
Hi baby, you OK? I miss you

                              K
I miss you too, where's Clee?

                            TROY
He went home

                              K
Oh well

                            VELT
What baby?

                              K
No; it's just that Wanda wanted to take
a nap, but it's OK, he misses his mommy

                            TROY
Mom can I go to Clee's house?

                            VELT
                          (smiling)
Yes! and call before you come back

                            TROY
OK

TROY RUNS OUT THE HOUSE IN EXCITEMENT. VELT PICKS
UP K AND HEADS FOR THE BEDROOM

                            VELT
Now can I show you how much I miss you?

IT'S TUESDAY EVENING, K IS ON THE COUCH WATCHING TV
AND EATING ICE-CREAM, THE PHONE RINGS AND ITS WANDA

                         WANDA
                    (speaking low)
K

                           K
What's going on girl, you're not
sounding too good

                         WANDA
I'm heading to the doctor, I've been
spotting all night, and he told me to
come in now

                           K
                    (sounding worried)
Oh no Wanda, the baby, are you in pain?
Do you want me to come with you?

                         WANDA
No, it's OK; I'll call you in a little
bit to let you know what's going on

                           K
Are you sure? I can come down now

                         WANDA
I'll call you

TWO HOURS HAVE PAST SINCE WANDA LEFT, K IS SITTING
ON THE COUCH WAITING FOR THE PHONE TO RING WHEN
TROY COMES IN AND DROPS HIS BOOK BAG ON THE FLOOR

                         TROY
What's up mom?

                    (rubbing K's stomach)
Hi Tre', what are you doing in there?

                         WANDA
Troy go tell Clee to come up stairs
until his mother gets home; and get
your book bag off the floor

TROY HURRIES TO THE DOOR AND CALLS FOR CLEE, WHO IS
STANDING AT HIS FRONT DOOR. CLEE RUSHES UPSTAIRS

                                    Mary J. Mckinney

CLEE

Troy can we play the game. Hi Ms. K, where's my mom

K

She had to run off; she should be back in a little while, you boys go do your homework

CLEE
(whispering to Troy)

Can we play the game when we're done?

TROY

My mom won't let us, not on a school night, but we can watch cartoons

CLEE

OK, we'll watch Scobby Doo

TROY AND CLEE FINISH THEIR HOMEWORK AND WATCH TV WHILE EATING LEFTOVERS FROM THE NIGHT BEFORE. THE PHONE RINGS AND K HURRIES TO ANSWER IT

K

Hello

WANDA

What's up girl, did Clee come up?

K

Yes he's here, what happened? Is the baby OK?

WANDA

Yes I'm still pregnant, but I have to chill out for a while. The doctor ran some test and made me an appointment for next week

K

So why were you bleeding?

WANDA

It's time for my cycle; he says that's common in the early stages of pregnancy for some women, plus I've been doing some things I shouldn't have

and stop coming up these stairs too

WANDA

OK momma

THERE'S A KNOCK AT THE DOOR

K

Hold on Wanda, somebody's at the door.
Who is it?

JAKE

It's me, Jake

K

*(speaking into the phone as she lays
it down)*

Jake, one moment please

(opening the door)

Hi Jake, what's up?

JAKE

(sounding desperate)

Have you seen Wanda? How is she?

K

I haven't seen her today, but she's fine

JAKE

K I'm sorry, I never meant to hurt her,
you know I love that girl. Could you
talk to her for me please K?

K

That's something you'll have to do, but
I will tell her you stopped by

JAKE

She won't return my phone calls

HEARING JAKE'S VOICE, CLEE RUSHES OUT THE ROOM

CLEE

Jake!

JAKE
(hugging)
What's up Clee, I miss you man

CLEE
I miss you too; momma said you moved
out, why? When are you coming back home?

JAKE
I don't know little man, ask your mother,
and tell her that I love her, OK

CLEE
OK, bye Jake

CLEE GIVES JAKE ANOTHER HUG AND GOES BACK IN THE
ROOM. K TURNS AWAY AS SHE SEES JAKE EYES FILL UP
WITH TEARS

JAKE
K please talk to her, I need my family
back

K
I'll tell her you came by

JAKE WALKS AWAY AND K CLOSE THE DOOR; SHE HURRIES
TO THE PHONE TO TALK TO WANDA, WHO HAS HUNG UP. SHE
CALLS WANDA back

K
(on the phone)
Girl the man looks bad, like he just
got robbed or something

WANDA
Good, his butt needs to suffer; I'm tired
of his ass

K
So you don't want him back?

WANDA
I don't know; my x has been looking
good these days, and he got a great job

                              K

You mean Rod or Benny

                           WANDA

Rod girl

                              K

I thought you were over him

                           WANDA

I was until a couple weeks ago; remember
when you didn't here from me all week

                              K
                      (sounding upset)

You were with Rod? I thought you stopped
cheating on Jake

                           WANDA

I tried, but he makes me so mad at
times; besides, he cheats on me too

                              K

Two wrongs don't make a right, you know
better than that Wanda and what about
the baby?

                           WANDA

I love Jake; don't get me wrong; I just
can't trust the man. I've always wanted
to have his baby, so I will, and I can
do that without him

                              K
                      (sounding angry)

Wanda I'm done talking to you on this
phone

K HANGS UP THE PHONE AND HEADS FOR THE KITCHEN WHEN
THE PHONE RINGS

                              K

What Wanda! I told you I don't want to
hear it

                            VELT
                    (sounding concerned)

Girl what's wrong with you?

                                    Mary J. Mckinney

K

Oh, sorry baby, I thought you were Wanda

VELT

and why are you yelling at Wanda

K

It's a long story, girl stuff. What are you up to? Working hard?

VELT

Just thinking about you, listen I don't want you getting upset baby

K

I miss you too, when are you coming home?

VELT

I'm on my way, you need anything?

K

just you baby

VELT

me, coming right up

IT'S A LOVELY SATURDAY, K AND WANDA ARE AT THE NEIGHBORHOOD PARK WATCHING CLEE AND TROY PLAY BASKETBALL WITH THE OTHER KIDS

WANDA

Are we going shopping today?

K

no, maybe tomorrow, I promised to take the boys to the movies

WANDA

oh yel

    (pausing to stare at a young man passing by)

I forgot

MAN

Hello ladies

                        WANDA & K

Hello

THE MAN WALKS TOWARDS THEM; HE'S ABOUT 6'1, ATHLETIC
BUILT, WITH HAZEL EYES; A REAL LADIES MAN. HE MAKES
SERIOUS EYE CONTACT WITH WANDA AS SHE STARES HIM UP
AND DOWN. HE SMILES AS HE PASS BY, HEADED FOR THE
WATER FOUNTAIN BEHIND THEM

                            K
                        (low tone)

Stop eye balling the man

                        WANDA

I can't help it, look at him

WANDA STANDS UP AS THE MAN LEAVES THE WATER FOUNTAIN

                        WANDA
                (extending her hand)

hello stranger, I'm Wanda, and this is
my friend K

                        MAN

Hi, I'm Jason

                        WANDA

So Jason, do you live around here?

                        JASON

No, I'm from North Carolina; just
visiting my little cuz before he goes
over seas, he's in the Army. You girls
live around here?

                        WANDA

Yes, right up the street

                        JASON

well listen, we're having a party later
tonight for my cousin, and if you girls
are not doing anything, you're welcome
to come

                        WANDA

that would be great!

WANDA HANDS JASON HER PHONE FOR HIM TO PUT IN HIS
NUMBER. JASON ENTERS HIS NUMBER AND HANDS THE PHONE
BACK TO HER

JASON

Call me around eight for the directions,
OK?

WANDA

You bet

JASON
(walking away backwards)

A pleasure meeting you both, I'll see
you later, I have to get back to my game

WANDA
(amazed, low voice)

I think I'm in love

K

Sit down, what's wrong with you?

WANDA

Damn K, he is so fine

AS WANDA SITS ON THE BENCH, JAKE, WHOM SHE DON'T
NOTICE, IS STANDING BEHIND HER

JAKE

and what am I?

BOTH GIRLS TURN AROUND AT THE SAME TIME, SHOCKED BY
THE VOICE THEY HEAR

WANDA

Jake! What are you doing here?

JAKE

looking for my love, but I see you're
busy trying to make new friends. Hello
K, Wanda can I talk to you for five
minutes please?

WANDA

we have nothing to talk about, it's over

JAKE

are you still carrying my baby?

WANDA
(in a rough tone)

Yes I'm still carrying my baby; it's
OK, and we don't need your help

JAKE

but I need you, Wanda I'm sorry, I was
wrong. Baby I love you and I want to be
a part of your life, please baby, don't
throw us away

WANDA

How many times have we been through
this Jake?

JAKE

Wanda it's not just me, you keep doing
me wrong and expect for me to put up
with it. I haven't done half the stuff
you do.

(tearful)

Is this what you want Wanda, for me to
be out of your life? Is this that you
really want?

WANDA

Yes, now leave me the hell alone

WANDA WALKS OFF FROM JAKE AND TAKE A SEAT NEXT TO
K ON THE BENCH; SHE DOESN'T LOOK BACK AT JAKE, WHO
IS STILL STANDING THERE

JAKE

I love you Wanda, I'll always love you.
We've hurt each other, and for the both
of us, I'm sorry. I'm leaving tomorrow;
call me when you go into labor please,
I would love to be there with you

JAKE HANDS HER A PIECE OF PAPER OVER HER SHOULDER,
AND WALKS AWAY. K IS LOOKING AT WANDA AS IF SHE
SHOULD BE STOPPING HIM

                        K

     Jake!

                      JAKE
               (turning around)

     Yes K

                        K

     Where are you going?

                      JAKE

     Carolina; I'm moving back home, there's
     nothing here for me anymore. Bye K,
     take care of my girl

JAKE WALKS AWAY

                        K

     Why didn't you say some thing Wanda?

                     WANDA

     What should I say K

                 (sarcastic tone)

     Oh Jake no, please baby come back

WANDA STANDS AND POINT IN THE DIRECTION OF THE
BASKETBALL COURT

                     WANDA

     I want that

                 (referring to Jason)

                        K
                  (angry tone)

     Come on, let's go

K YELLS OUT FOR THE BOYS TO COME AS THEY HEAD
TOWARDS THE PARKING LOT, TOP THE CAR

                     WANDA

     K; why are you upset with me? You know
     how Jake is; he's a whore

K

and so are you; you made the man like that Wanda. Do you remember how he use to be home babysitting while we were at the club all the time? You would leave before me, and still wouldn't get home till after 10am.

How long did you expect the poor guy to put up with your mess Wanda? He did because he wanted to be with you that much.

WANDA

Why you bringing up old stuff?

K

It's not that old to him; hell you still do it, just not ass much. I just want you to realize what you have before you throw it all away for nothing

WANDA

I had nothing, his paycheck barely paid the bills; my son's child support check is what kept us afloat.

CLEE AND TROY RACE TO THE CAR AND ALMOST KNOCK WANDA TO THE GROUND

CLEE

I beat! You're a rotten egg

(referring to Troy)

TROY

No; you took off before the count, cheater

K

get in, you guys have to take a shower, the movie starts at 7:30 sharp

WANDA

and I have a party to get to

THEY ALL GET IN THE CAR AND HEAD FOR HOME.

Mary J. Mckinney

IT'S MONDAY MORNING; K AND WANDA ARE DOWN STAIRS SEEING THE BOYS OFF TO SCHOOL. A NEIGHBOR PASSING BY NOTICING K"S BELLY

NEIGHBOR

girl, you're getting huge

K
(smiling)

What's up girl?

NEIGHBOR

Nothing, big girl. Hi Wanda

WANDA

Hi Sandy

WANDA'S HOUSE PHONE BEGINS TO RING

K

Are you going to get that?

WANDA

They'll leave a message. So what's up for later? Let's go to the Mall, I need some maternity clothes

K

For what? You only weight 100pds. You're not even showing. And where the hell have you been all weekend?

WANDA

I called you Saturday night from the party, remember?

K

You told me you'd be home in a couple hours, not a couple days. Clee was also worried about you Wanda. You got to stop doing this.

WANDA

I had to take Jason to the airport after dinner yesterday

                              K

so that's where you were? Wanda, I'm so
disappointed in you

                           WANDA

For what?

                              K

For sleeping with a stranger

                           WANDA

But K, he's not just any stranger, he's
a professional basketball player; and
yes we were very careful

                              K

very careful, did you use condoms

                           WANDA

Yes, at first. We ran out of condoms the
second night, but he pulled out

                              K
                    (shaking her head)

You just won't listen, will you? So
what you're saying is, you didn't catch
a disease the first night, but you're
not sure about the second night

                           WANDA

He pulled out K. stop worrying about
me so much; I'm a blessed child, I'll
be OK

        (headed for the ringing phone)

Let me get this, it might be Kurt's
cousin; I missed two calls from him
yesterday

K TURNS TO WALK AWAY AS SHES SHAKING HER HEAD IN
DISBELIEF

                              K

I'll see you later girl, call me when
you got sense, after my talk shows go
off

Mary J. Mckinney

WANDA

OK

(answering the phone)

Hello, hello

SECRETARY

Hello, may I speak to Ms. Wanda Brown
please

WANDA

Yes, this is she

SECRETARY

Hi Ms. Brown, this is Dr. Moore's
secretary, and he would like to see you
at his office today; can you come in this
morning?

WANDA

Is everything OK?

(sounding worried)

What's wrong?

SECRETARY

The Doctor will speak with you when you
get in

WANDA

sure, I'll be there as soon as I get
dressed

SECRETARY

Thank you mam, I'll let Dr. Moore know
you're coming

WANDA HANGS UP THE PHONE AND CALLS K

WANDA

K, it's me

K

I thought I told you not to bother me
until after "Maury" goes off

WANDA

Shut up and listen. I'm headed to the
Doctor; he wants to check the baby.
I'll call you on my way home so we can
go to the mall, OK?

K

well I guess I can use the exercise,
but ask the Doctor if it's OK for you
to walk so much

WANDA

too late, I've been dancing and walking
all weekend

K

Speaking of weekend, did you tell your
new boyfriend that you're expecting?

WANDA

That's none of his business

K

Bye Wanda, call me later

K WATCHES TV ALL MORNING BEFORE FALLING TO SLEEP
ON THE COUCH. SHE IS AWAKENED BY THE SOUND OF KIDS
PLAYING OUTSIDE. TROY KNOCKS ON THE DOOR, K GET'S
UP TO OPEN IT. TROY GIVES HER A BIG HUG THEN PULLS
A PAPER STAR FROM HIS POCKET AND HANDS IT TO HER

TROY

momma I had a good day at school today,
I received the "Great Leader Star"

K

(hugging)

Baby I'm so proud of you; you're going
to be the best big brother in the world.
Change out your school clothes, and
I'll take you for some ice-cream

TROY

OK!

K AND TROY RETURN HOME AFTER 7PM; THEY WERE GONE
LONGER THAN EXPECTED BECAUSE THEY DECIDED TO HAVE

DINNER WHILE THEY WERE OUT. VELT IS GETTING OUT OF
HIS CAR AS THEY PULL INTO THE APARTMENT COMPLEX.
TROY RUNS OVER TO GREET VELT

TROY

Hi Velt!

VELT

What up my big man how was school today?

TROY
(excited tone)

tell him mom; tell Velt what I got in
school today

K
(smiling)

my big man got a "Leadership Star" for
being such a great leader

VELT

Good Troy! I'm proud of you; that's
exactly what we need, more leaders

K HANDS VELT THE BAG SHE HAS IN HERE HAND

K

here baby, we brought you something
back

VELT

What is it?

TROY

your favorite

VELT
(sniffing the bag)

Ahh ribs

THE FAMILY OF THREE HEAD UPSTAIRS. K NOTICE WANDA'S
CAR AND REALIZE THAT THEY DIDN'T MAKE IT TO THE MALL
TODAY. SHE CALLS WANDA WHEN SHE GETS IN THE HOUSE,
BUT CLEE ANSWERS AND SAYS SHE'S IN THE SHOWER

BY MORNING IT'S VERY CLOUDY. K IS DOWN STAIRS WITH
TROY AT THE BUS STOP; CLEE WALKS UP TO JOIN THEM
LOOKING SAD AND RESTLESS

                         K
        Good morning Clee

                        CLEE
                 (speaking slowly)
        good morning Ms. K, what's up Troy

                         K
                   (concerned)
        What's wrong Clee? What is your mom
        doing?

                        CLEE
        She's still in the bathroom throwing
        up; she's been in there all night

                         K
        I'll see you guys later, have a good
        day

K GIVES BOTH BOYS A HUG BEFORE RUSHING OFF TO
WANDA'S DOOR. SHE KNOCK BUT GETS NO ANSWER, SO SHE
WALKS IN

                         K
        Wanda!

                       WANDA
        I'm in here!

WANDA YELLS FROM THE BATHROOM AS K REACHES THE
BATHROOM DOOR. THE DOOR IS LOCKED, K LEANS ON THE
DOOR

                         K
        What's wrong?

                       WANDA
        I've been sick all night; I can't take
        this; I want an abortion

                           K
                       (shocked)

What! Wanda, open this door! Wanda!

WANDA OPENS THE DOOR LOOKING A MESS. SHE LOOKS AT
K AND BEGIN CRYING UNCONTROLLABLY. K EMBRACE HER

                           K

Wanda calm down, it'll be OK; come sit
down and I'll fix you some soup and
crackers, that'll make you feel better

                        WANDA
                    (walking away)

No! That won't help me

                           K
                      (confused)

Wanda, what is wrong with you? What are
you talking about?

WANDA TURNS TO FACE K

                        WANDA

I'm dying K, I'm going to die

                           K
                       (upset)

Wanda please stop scaring me, what the
hell are you talking about?

                        WANDA
                       (crying)

I'm HIV Positive, that's what the doctor
wanted to see me about; my blood work
says I'm dying

K IS DEVASTATED, THEY HUG EACH OTHER AND CRY TOGETHER

TWO HOURS HAVE PAST AND K IS STILL DOWN STAIRS AT
WANDA'S APARTMENT. WANDA IS SOAKING IN A HOT BUBBLE
BATH TO HELP CALM HER DOWN, AND K IS IN THE FRONT
ROOM ON THE COUCH READING PAMPHLETS ON HIV/AIDS,
PREGNANT WITH HIV, HIV COUNSELING INFO; WHATEVER

SHE CAN TO SAVE HER FRIEND.SHE IS CRYING SILENTLY
AS BAD THOUGHTS ENTER HER MIND. K DOESN'T WANT TO
LOSE HER BEST-FRIEND, WHOM SHE LOVES LIKE A SISTER

WANDA CALLS OUT TO K FROM THE BATHROOM

WANDA

K!

K

Yes Wanda

WANDA

I can't have this baby, as much as I
want to, I can't

(crying silently)

I don't want a child that is going to
be sick all the time and I can't do
anything about it; that would hurt me
so bad, I can't do that to the baby

K WALKS IN THE BATHROOM WITH A PAMPHLET AND SITS
DOWN ON THE TOILET

K

Yes you can Wanda, your baby has a very
good chance of surviving this, and you
will be around to raise your own child

WANDA

I am HIV positive K, how many people you
know of, have survived this? remember
Kurt, where is he

(crying)

This is the worst K, I don't know what
to do, and Clee; oh my little man. K
promise me that you will take Clee, he
loves you and Troy. Please...

K INTERRUPTS WANDA IN AN ANGRY TONE

K

Wanda chill out! You

Are not dead, and as strong a woman as
you are, you will not let this defeat
you; now get out of this tub and let's
go to this class that the doctor insist
you attend. I mean it Wanda, I'm going
to get dressed, be ready when I get back

WANDA

OK

K

I won't lose you to this Wanda; I love
you girl

K GOES TO HER APARTMENT, GET DRESSED, AND HER AND
WANDA HEAD TO THE "LIVENING WITH HIV/AIDS" CLASS

AFTER SPENDING ALMOST 3 HOURS IN CLASS, THE GIRLS
HEAD HOME FEELING SO MUCH BETTER AND VERY HOPEFUL

WANDA

Could you believe that beautiful young
woman has been positive for 8 years?

K

and she's had two children since then

WANDA

those people looked great, none of
them looked sick, most of them are
undetectable

K

It's going to be OK Wanda, and the baby
is going to be OK too

WANDA

thank you K, I'm glad you made me go to
the class. I now know that HIV is not
the death sentence, and I plan to live
my life to the fullest

K
(*low tone*)

So what about Jake, remember, you have
to tell him. He needs to be tested

WANDA

I wish I could K, but I don't know how.
Maybe he already knows, maybe he gave
it to me, maybe...

K
(interrupting)

Wanda, let's not get in a negative
mind-state; remember what is important
right now. Your health is what we're
dealing with, and you have an obligation
to inform those who you have come in
contact with unprotected, OK?

WANDA

you're right K. I should have been
protecting myself, it's nobody's fault
but mine; just as the people I have
been with, should have been protecting
themselves. No 10 or 15 minutes of
pleasure is worth this K. you were right
to be upset when Velt cheated on you,
because you are so aware of the dangers
of unprotected sex. I'm so sorry for
thinking that you were over-reacting
and being too hard on him

K

Its ok girl; you hungry? Because I'm
starving

THE GIRLS STOP BY A NEAR-BY RESTAURANT TO GRAB A
BITE TO EAT BEFORE HEADING HOME.

WANDA WAKES UP EARLY THE NEXT MORNING HOPING THE
DAY BEFORE WAS JUST A NIGHTMARE, BUT SHE REALIZE IT
WASN'T, AFTER SEEING THE AIDS PAMPHLETS K LEFT IN
THE BATHROOM. HER EYES SUDDENLY FILLED WITH TEARS
AS SHE BRUSH HER TEETH AND WASH HER FACE. SHE HEARS
A KNOCK AT THE DOOR AND WASHES HER FACE AGAIN SO K
WON'T SEE HER CRYING.

WANDA
(yelling out)

coming K, yes I'm still alive!

WANDA OPENS THE DOOR AND IS VERY SURPRISED TO SEE
JAKE STANDING THERE

                    JAKE
        Hi baby, I'm sorry I need you, can you
        please forgive me baby

                    WANDA
        Jake, what are you doing here?

                    JAKE
        begging for my family. I have something
        for you

JAKE GETS DOWN ON BENDED KNEES RIGHT IN THE DOORWAY,
AND PULLS A BLACK RING CASE FROM HIS BACK POCKET.
HE OPENS THE CASE AND THE STUNNING DIAMOND ALMOST
BLINDS WANDA, AS SHE LOOKS MESMERIZED

                    JAKE
        Wanda please give me a chance to be the
        best man I can be. Give me a chance to
        be a part of your life; this is all I'll
        ever need. I've never loved a woman as
        much as I love you, and I never will

                    WANDA
        Jake please

                    (crying)

        Jake I don't know...

                    JAKE
                  (interrupting)

        Wanda please don't say no. If you need
        time to think about it, I'll give you
        15 minutes.

WANDA WALKS IN THE FRONT-ROOM AND SIT DOWN ON
THE COUCH, JAKE FOLLOWS HER. WANDA BEGINS TO CRY
UNCONTROLLABLY

                    WANDA
        Jake

JAKE

Wanda, what is it? What's wrong?

JAKE SITS ON THE COUCH AND HOLDS WANDA AS SHE CRY
UNCONTROLLABLY IN HIS ARMS

WANDA

I received some very bad news from the
doctor the other day Jake

JAKE

No Wanda, is the baby OK

WANDA

Yes, the baby is fine, it's me

JAKE
(concerned look)

What baby, what's wrong

WANDA
(crying)

I'm sick Jake

JAKE

Sick

WANDA

Yes, I'm HIV positive

JAKE

WHAT! NO, No Wanda, No

JAKE BEGINS TO CRY AS HE KEEPS REPEATING THE WORD
"NO" WANDA HANDS HIM HER FOLDER SHE RECEIVED AT THE
HIV CLASS. JAKE REFUSES TO TAKE IT, BUT WANDA INSISTS

WANDA

I was thinking about getting rid of the
baby, until K made me attend this class
yesterday. The baby has a 99% chance of
being born HIV negative.

JAKE
(crying)

and you? what about me?

WANDA

I can live a long healthy life, I just have to take care of myself much better and take my meds. You Jake, you have to get tested right away

JAKE

Oh my God

(holding his head)

Oh my God

WANDA

It's OK Jake, I won't hold you to anything you said earlier, you are not obligated to be with me, I just want you to get tested and be OK

JAKE LOOK AT WANDA AS HE WIPES THE TEARS FROM HIS EYES; HE GETS ON HIS KNEES AND SLIDES THE RING ON WANDA'S FINGER

JAKE

Wanda I am obligated to love you for the rest of my life, no disease in the world can stop me from loving you as much as I do right now. You are my queen Wanda; will you make me the happiest man in the world by becoming my wife?

WANDA
(crying silently)

are you sure you want me?

JAKE

yes baby, I need you, I need my family

WANDA

yes Jake, yes baby

JAKE
(kissing)

I miss you so much

WANDA

Where have you been staying?

JAKE

With Luther; where's Clee?

WANDA

He stayed upstairs at K's. Let's go get
your things before he gets here, he'll
be so surprised

JAKE

OK, let's go

WANDA LEAVES A NOTE ON THE DOOR SAYING SHE'LL BE
BACK IN 20 MINUTES. SHE RIDES WITH JAKE TO LUTHER'S
HOUSE. JAKE AGREES TO GET TESTED ON MONDAY, AFTER
A SMALL CHURCH WEDDING ON SUNDAY.

JAKE AND WANDA ARRIVE BACK AT THE COMPLEX JUST AS
CLEE IS WALKING AWAY FROM THEIR APARTMENT DOOR

CLEE
(surprised)

Jake!

CLEE RUNS AT FULL SPEED AND JUMPS IN JAKE'S ARMS

JAKE
(laughing)

Clee, what's up big guy, I miss you

CLEE

I miss you too Jake, are you coming
back home?

JAKE

if that's OK with you

CLEE

All right! mom Jake is coming home

WANDA

Yes he is baby, and Jake has something
to ask you

CLEE

What is it Jake?

JAKE

I was wondering if you would be OK with
me marring your mother

CLEE
(excited)

Does that mean we'll always be a family,
you won't leave anymore?

JAKE

That's right Clee; I'll be the man of
the house

CLEE

Great! I was tired of being the man
anyway. I'm so glad you came back

JAKE

I'm so glad to be back Clee. Now help
me get my things out the car

CLEE

OK dad

CLEE AND JAKE BOTH LAUGH AS THEY HEAD TO THE CAR.

K STEPS OUTSIDE HER DOOR LOOKING FOR CLEE, SHE SEES
WANDA

K

Girl where you just coming from this
early in the morning? Did you see Clee?

WANDA

Yes, he's helping Jake get his things
out the car

K
(surprised)

Huh?

JAKE

Hi K

K

Hi Jake, so good to see you

                            JAKE
          So good to be seen, how are you doing?

                             K

          fine, thank you

WANDA MOVES OUT THE DOORWAY TO LET JAKE AND CLEE
COME THROUGH WITH JAKE'S THINGS

                           WANDA
          I'll be up when I put these clothes up

                             K
                          (smiling)

          take your time girl. Clee had his
          breakfast already

                           WANDA
          OK, I'll see you in a little bit

AN HOUR HAS PAST BY AND WANDA IS AT K'S DOOR

                             K
          Come in girl, the door is open!

WANDA COMES IN AND CHANGE THE TV CHANNEL AS SHE
SITS DOWN ON THE COUCH

                           WANDA
          K, did you watch the Stories lately

                             K
          No, I'm sick of Brook

                           WANDA
          Me too

K COMES FROM THE ROOM AND SIT DOWN ON THE COUCH
BESIDE WANDA. SHE SMILES AS SHE GIVES HER A HUG

                             K
          So what's going on girl; how did Jake
          end up moving back in so fast?

                           WANDA
          I woke up thinking yesterday was a

                                  Mary J. Mckinney

dream, then Jake knocked at the door;
I thought it was you checking up on me

                    K

did you tell him?

                  WANDA

Yes, it was the hardest thing I ever had
to do K; he was in such shock because he
had just begged me to marry him seconds
before.

                    K

So he's OK; is he going to get tested?

                  WANDA

Yes Monday, after the wedding Sunday at
church

                    K

What wedding

                  WANDA

K, will you please be my Maid of Horner

                    K

Oh my God Wanda, are you serious

                  WANDA

well Jake is calling his Pastor to ask
if we can have a quick ceremony after
church Sunday

                  JAKE

Wanda! Wanda!

THE GIRLS HEAR JAKE YELLING FROM DOWN STAIRS, THEY
BOTH RUSH TO THE DOOR

                  JAKE

He said yes baby! you're going to be my
wife Sunday at 3pm

                  WANDA
                 (crying)

Oh Jake, I love you

JAKE

I love you too girl

WANDA TURNS TO HUG K, WHO IS CRYING ALSO. K'S BELLY
GETS IN THE WAY OF THE HUG

WANDA

Well what's the answer big girl, will
you?

K

Of course I will Wanda, if I hold up
that long. I'm so happy for you; I love
you girl

TROY

Hi Ms. Wanda

WANDA

Hi Troy, where you just come from

TROY

out the shower, my mom is going to take
us skating and out to lunch today, so
tell Clee to be ready at 2:00

WANDA

OK Troy, and what is the reason you
guys are out of school again today

TROY

It's Teacher's Work Day, so we have a
long weekend

WANDA

I see; you kids are out of school more
than you are in

TROY

I have to go get fresh because all our
friends will be at the skating-rink
today. Tell Clee to come back up when
he gets dressed

WANDA

OK, he's down stairs with Jake, I'll
tell him...

TROY
(Interrupting)

What! Jake is down there; never mind
I'm going down

TROY RUSH OFF TO HIS ROOM TO GET DRESSED

K

It seems the kids miss Jake more than
anyone does

WANDA
(laughing)

He does love the kids, and he can't
wait to be a father

K

speaking of father's, are you going to
call yours to tell him you're getting
married

WANDA

No, I haven't spoke to that man since
my mother's funeral

K

I think you should call him Wanda, he
does love you; besides, who's going to
give you away?

WANDA

Velt

K
(surprised)

Velt!

WANDA

Yes, I feel he is the best man for the
job, and I know he'll be glad to give
me away

THE GIRLS BEGIN TO LAUGH

IT'S 6PM, K AND THE BOYS HAVE JUST COME BACK FROM

THE SKATING-RINK. CLEE WALKS TO HIS DOOR AND WAVES
GOODNIGHT AS THE DOOR OPENS; JAKE SAYS THANKS TO K

TROY
thanks mom, that was fun

K
Yel, well I'm tired, you boys have worn
me out

TROY
I'll be glad when my little brother
gets here

K
Me to Troy, the doctor said any day now

K AND TROY ENTER THEIR APARTMENT, VELT IS IN THE
SHOWER. HE HAS LEFT-OVERS WARMING ON THE STOVE
BECAUSE HE KNEW K WAS TAKING THE BOYS OUT TODAY.
TROY WATCHES TV AS HE WAITS TO TAKE A SHOWER. K
HEADS TO THE KITCHEN TO FIX VELT'S FOOD FOR HIM

IT'S SUNDAY MORNING AND EVERYONE IS GETTING READY
FOR THE WEDDING. JAKE'S MOTHER AND SISTER FLEW IN
FROM CAROLINA YESTERDAY. JAKE'S MOM LOOKS LIKE SHE
CAN BE HIS SISTER, SHE'S BEAUTIFUL. K IS UPSET THAT
SHE LOOKS TOO BIG TO BE A MAID OF HONOR, BUT WANDA
DOESN'T WANT TO HEAR IT. JAKE IS SO HANDSOME IN HIS
WHITE TUX AND WANDA LOOKS STUNNING, HER BELLY POKES
OUT SO CUTE UNDER HER BEAUTIFUL GOWN THAT JAKE'S
MOTHER WORE ON HER WEDDING DAY. TROY AND CLEE LOOK
LIKE TWO LITTLE MEN WITH THERE FRESH HAIR CUTS,
AND VELT IS CLEAN ENOUGH TO BE THE GROOM HIMSELF.
EVERYONE HEADS FOR THE LIMO THAT IS WAITING OUTSIDE

K
Are you nervous little girl?

WANDA
A little, oh K, I am so happy, thank you
for being my friend

K
I have a gift for you

WANDA

Where is it

K

later

THE WEDDING IS ABOUT TO TAKE PLACE AND IT SEEMS
THAT ALL THE MEMBERS DECIDED TO STAY AFTER FOR
THE WEDDING. WANDA WALKS DOWN THE ILES WITH SUCH
CONFIDENCE, SHE IS SO BEAUTIFUL. AS SHE APPROACHES
THE FRONT OF THE CHURCH HER VEIL IS LIFTED BY...

MR. BROWN

You are as lovely as your mother was

WANDA

Dad

WANDA LOOKS OVER AT K, WHO KNODS HER HEAD FOR WANDA
TO ACCEPT HER GIFT. WANDA SMILES IN ACCEPTANCE AS
SHE TRIES REALLY HARD TO HOLD BACK HER TEARS. HER
FATHER LOOKS SO GOOD; SHE IS VERY PLEASED WITH
HIS APPEARANCE. THE CEREMONY CONTINUES AS LUTHER
CLEARS HIS THOUGH, HE TOO LOOKS STUNNING AS HE
STANDS BE SIDE JAKE

WANDA

I DO

PASTOR

I now pronounce you husband and wife,
you may kiss your bride

K
(yelling out)

Oh! Oh!

VELT

What is it baby?

K

I think we're going to have a wedding
and a baby on the same day!

JAKE

I'll get the car!

K

I'm sorry Wanda; you guys enjoy the
rest of your wedding day

WANDA

Are you crazy, we're taking this party
to the hospital; this is defiantly a day
to remember

THE ENTIRE WEDDING PARTY REACHES THE HOSPITAL IN
10 MINUTES. THE HOSPITAL STAFF RUSH K INTO THE
DELIVERY ROOM, VELT IS RIGHT BEHIND THEM. WANDA AND
HER DAD HOLD A WELL OVER-DUE CONVERSATION, WHILE
THE REST OF THE PARTY LAUGHS AND JOKE AS TIME PASS
QUICKLY BY.

THE NURSE WALK UP TO THE CROWD WITH THE GOOD NEWS
OF A HEALTHY 8 POUND BABY BOY.

WANDA

Hi Nurse Nicky

NURSE NICKY

Hi Wanda, how are you?

WANDA

OK and you?

NURSE NICKY

Wow, I see you have a gift in front of
you, you look beautiful, congratulations

WANDA

Thank you, Nurse Nicky, can I speak
with you in private for a minute

NURSE NICKY

sure Wanda

WANDA AND NURSE NICKY WALK DOWN THE HALL AND INTO
HER OFFICE. WANDA TELLS NURSE NICKY ABOUT HER TEST
RESULTS AND THE NEED FOR HER HUSBAND TO BE TESTED.
NURSE NICKY INSURES WANDA THAT SHE WILL BE OK.
SHE MAKES AN APPOINTMENT FOR JAKE TOMORROW MORNING
AFTER THEY DROP HIS FAMILY OFF AT THE AIRPORT.

IT'S ABOUT 11AM WHEN WANDA AND JAKE REACH THE HOSPITAL. THEY BOTH GO TO SEE HOW K IS FEELING. THE BABY IS IN THE ROOM AND SO IS VELT

K

Hi Wanda, Hi Jake, come see your God Child

WANDA

Oh look at him, he's a big guy

K

He's a Jr.

WANDA

Oh no, not another one of him

VELT

It's OK Wanda, I know you're madly in love with me and you just don't know how to express yourself. Just tell me Wanda, I'll let you down easy

WANDA

I'm so glad he looks like K, because I couldn't take another cross-eyed Velt

EVERYONE LAUGHS BUT VELT

VELT

Baby you shouldn't laugh at animal talk. Come on Jake; walk with me to get some coffee

JAKE

OK Velt, I could use some. You two have a beautiful baby boy; now I'll have a boy and a girl. Thank you for allowing me to be Lil Velt's God Father

VELT

Come on man, don't be getting all mussy on me; you're not going to cry are you?

JAKE

no, not if you get me out of here

VELT

Let's go

VELT AND JAKE WALK DOWN THE HALL TOWARDS THE
CAFETERIA. K HANDS WANDA THE BABY

WANDA

Oh K, he is beautiful, he looks like
the both of you

K

He sure was ready to come in this world.
Troy took 13 hours to get here; this
guy came in less than an hour

WANDA

I pray my labor will be over that fast

K

Keep praying

WANDA

Jake is going to have his test done
here today

K

How is he, is he OK with it?

WANDA

He just wants to be with me K; I've
never felt so loved. Clee came in the
room this morning and gave him a big
hug before going to the bus-stop. I
see now what Jake had been trying to
tell me from day one; all he wants is a
family that he can love, and that loves
him back, I do love him K, I really do

K

Good, he deserves that. I'm so proud of
you Wanda, I really am

WANDA

I'm going to be OK, I realize people
die every day from car accidents, gun
shots, cancer, all kinds of things; we
must be thankful for every day we have
on this earth

Mary J. Mckinney

K

That's right Wanda

THE BABY IS FAST ASLEEP IN WANDA'S ARMS; SHE LAYS
HIM DOWN TO SLEEP IN THE BASSINET BESIDE K'S BED.
VELT AND JAKE WALK INTO THE ROOM SIPPING ON THEIR
COFFEE

JAKE

I come to take my wife for a few minutes,
if that's OK with you K

K

Take her, take her

JAKE

This shouldn't take long, we'll be back
shortly

K

I maybe gone home soon, but check back
before you leave

VELT

Good luck man

JAKE

Thanks Velt

WANDA AND JAKE WALK DOWN THE HALL TOWARDS THE LAB,
THEY STOP AT THE DOOR

WANDA

Bless you Baby, I love you and I pray
you're OK

JAKE

I love you too Wanda, and no matter
what the results are, I plan to spend
the rest of my life with you, Clee, and
our beautiful baby girl

JAKE AND WANDA SHARE A PASSIONATE KISS BEFORE HE
SLIPS OFF INTO THE LAB FOR TESTING